stamp it!

stamp it!

DIY Printing with Handmade Stamps

jenny doh

LARK CRAFTS
Asheville

13 August 07
B+T
1995 (1217)

LARK CRAFTS

An Imprint of Sterling Publishing
387 Park Avenue South
New York, NY 10016

ISBN 978-1-4547-0399-0

Doh, Jenny.
    Stamp it! : DIY printing with handmade stamps / Jenny Doh. -- 1st ed.
        p. cm.
    Includes bibliographical references and index.
    ISBN 978-1-4547-0399-0
    1. Rubber stamp printing. I. Title.
    TT867.D64 2013
    761--dc23
            2012030626

Distributed in Canada by Sterling Publishing
c/o Canadian Manda Group, 165 Dufferin Street
Toronto, Ontario, Canada M6K 3H6
Distributed in the United Kingdom by GMC Distribution Services
Castle Place, 166 High Street, Lewes, East Sussex, England BN7 1XU
Distributed in Australia by Capricorn Link (Australia) Pty. Ltd.
P.O. Box 704, Windsor, NSW 2756, Australia

For information about custom editions, special sales, and premium and corporate purchases, please contact
Sterling Special Sales at 800-805-5489 or specialsales@sterlingpublishing.com.

Email academic@larkbooks.com for information about desk and examination copies.
The complete policy can be found at larkcrafts.com.

Manufactured in China

2   4   6   8   10   9   7   5   3   1

larkcrafts.com

contents

Basics

Welcome to *Stamp It*! The world of rubberstamping widens horizons for any artist, whether you're a crafter, a sewer, a painter, or a woodcarver. With a single stamp, you can customize stationery, embellish a tote bag, create a card, or personalize wrapping paper. You can design wedding invitations, print on T-shirts, or make unique placemats for your kids. You don't have to take a single art class or know how to sketch. All you need is a stamp, ink, and a surface.

If you want to take stamping even further, you can carve your own stamps using just a few simple tools, such as an eraser and a craft knife. Carving your own stamps makes your artwork that much more personal, and it allows you to use that unique image you've created in countless projects. This is the perfect excuse to make matching shirts, hats, and totes for everyone you know, don't you think?

Whether you choose to carve your own stamps, use purchased stamps, or even stamp using found objects, this book will teach you the ins and outs of this versatile art form. With so many variations on stamping, you will never get tired of the magic that comes from a rubber stamp.

gather

One of the joys of stamping lies in how quick and easy it is. With a few supplies and a basic knowledge of the craft, you'll be creating stamped art in no time. To the right is a list of basic supplies you'll need in your stamping tool kit; you'll use these supplies for the projects in this book, so you'll want to have them on hand.

carving tools

The most common tool used to carve a stamp is a linoleum cutter, such as the one made by Speedball. You can buy the linoleum cutter as a set, which comes with the linoleum cutter handle and a handful of attachments. The attachments are numbered, from No. 1 to No. 6, and vary in size, with No. 1 being the smallest and No. 5 being the biggest. They vary in shape as well; for example, No. 2 is shaped more like a V and No. 5 is shaped more like a U. No. 6 is shaped like a small knife. You will use different attachments depending on what the size of the stamp you're carving is and what texture you wish to create. Use the V-shaped blades to make lines and detail cuts and the U or round tips to scoop out the areas you don't want to print when you stamp. Experiment with the various blades on an eraser or a piece of linoleum to see what type of cut each tip produces.

If you don't have access to a linoleum cutter, you can also use a sharp craft knife. It will be harder to carve out small details, but if you're working on a larger shape, a craft knife will work.

basic stamping kit

- Translucent paper
- Pencil
- Rubber for carving
- Linoleum cutter and blades
- Sharp craft knife
- Inkpads
- Acrylic paints
- Scissors
- Paper towels

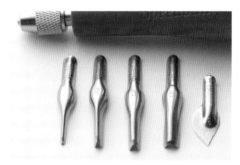

Linoleum cutter and blades No. 1 through No. 5.

The shape of the blade will determine the type of cut it'll deliver.

safety

The blades that are used with a linoleum cutter are extremely sharp. To ensure that you don't accidentally cut yourself, always push the cutter away from you rather than pulling it toward you. Do not use the tool on materials other than those that are intended to be carved with the blades. Provide close supervision when children are using carving tools.

carving blocks

You have several options for carving blocks, ranging from a common pink eraser to a soft rubber block designed for printmaking. Pink erasers are inexpensive, readily available, and carve beautifully, but are small in size. Just make sure the image you choose fits the eraser's space. You could also use the eraser at the end of a pencil to carve a cute and simple shape, say a mini heart or a star. Double-sided foam tape or just foam can be carved as well.

If you'd like to explore options specifically meant for carving stamps, try an artist carving block, such as a Martin Universal Moo Carve block or a Speedball Speedy-Carve block (which is also sold in a kit with a linoleum cutter included). These high-density rubber blocks come in a variety of sizes, allowing you to choose the one that works best for the project you have in mind.

Both pencil erasers and rubber blocks work well as carving substrates.

inks

The inks you apply to the stamps are what give stamped artwork color and life. Liquid inks can be used to color a stamp or the paper surface, while inkpads are most commonly used to load stamps with color before stamping. Many different types of inks exist, the most popular of which are listed below. Have fun experimenting with all of them to find your favorites.

- Pigment inks are thick in consistency and when stamped on paper, the ink will closely match the color on the inkpad. The ink colors are vibrant and fade-resistant. Rather than absorbing into paper, pigment ink stays mostly on top of the paper so it won't dry on glossy paper unless heat-set with an embossing gun.

- Dye inks dry quickly and are thinner in consistency than pigment inks. The final colors they produce are lighter than the color of the inkpad. Dye inks absorb into the paper so it can be used on any type of paper. Although acid-free, dye inks fade over time, especially when exposed to sunlight.

- Alcohol inks, such as Tim Holtz Adirondack by Ranger, are acid-free, permanent inks intended for use on glossy or other non-porous surfaces. They are packaged in bottles and can be used straight or diluted with water. These inks are more frequently blended together to create interesting backgrounds, rather than used to color one stamp.

- Solvent-based inks, such as StazOn by Tsukineko, are inkpads with permanent ink designed for use on non-porous surfaces. They will stick without the need for embossing.

- Acrylic paint is a common medium that stampers use to create a unique effect. Paint adds more texture to artwork than inkpads, and the colors remain vibrant even when dry.

- Fabric-friendly inks and paints such as VersaCraft inkpads by Tsukineko and Lumiere paints by Jacquard, are intended for use on fabric. They are thick, opaque enough to show up on fabric, and can be heat-set and washed.

re-inking tip

When an inkpad runs dry, many stampers find it much more economical to buy ink refills to re-ink their pads, rather than buying new inkpads. Re-inkers are small plastic bottles filled with ink and are sold by most major inkpad companies. To re-ink your inkpad, follow manufacturer's label to squeeze enough ink from the bottle so that the ink spreads evenly onto the inkpad.

make

Creating with purchased stamps can be fun, but many crafters find designing and making their own stamps extremely satisfying. The process is simple and outlined below.

carving

You'll be carving a stamp in many of the projects in this book. This section will teach you the basics of carving so you'll be ready to dive into whatever project appeals to you.

1 Find your desired image and trace it onto translucent paper with a pencil. All templates for all the projects are located in the back of the book, starting on page 130 (figs. A & B.).

2 Turn the translucent paper over and position it on an eraser or carving block (fig. C). Rub the image onto the eraser by burnishing the back of the paper with the side of a pencil (fig. D). If you prefer, you could draw freehand directly onto the eraser; just keep in mind that whatever is carved on the block will be a mirror image when stamped on paper. By drawing first on paper, then turning the paper over to transfer the image to the block, you are already reversing the image so it will come out right on paper (fig. E).

fig. A

fig. B

fig. C

finding images

When you're looking for images to turn into stamps, don't limit yourself. Simple shapes you can draw, fun images you find online, and even family pictures can all be good subject matter for a stamp. If you find a complicated image that may be hard to trace onto translucent paper, such as a family picture, another option for turning it into a carve-able image is to use Photoshop.

In Photoshop, use selection tools to remove the background. Then use the stamp filter to transform the image into an image you can carve. You may need to darken or lighten certain areas of the stamp to make them show up better. You can also resize the image in Photoshop, which is particularly useful when your stamp needs to be a specific size.

fig. D

fig. E

fig. F

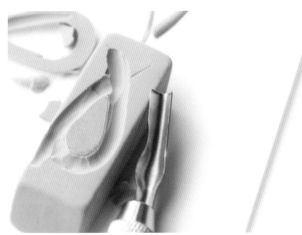

fig. G

fig. H

3 Hold the linoleum cutter like a pencil and apply pressure to the eraser (fig. F). Some artists like to begin with the small details first to ensure they'll have room for them; others like to begin with the major outlines to form a general idea of what the image is going to look like (fig. G). Try it both ways, and see what works best for you.

4 As you begin to carve, make sure you know which parts of the image you're going to carve away. The raised portion of the image is what's going to show up as a stamp. You'll need to decide if you want your stamped image to be a solid shape (where you *won't* cut out the center) or just the outline of a shape (where you *will* cut out the center).

5 Experiment with the different attachments to the linoleum cutter to find which sizes and shapes work best for the image. A good place to start is to carve the major outlines with the No. 5 cutter and the smaller details with the No. 1 cutter.

6 Once you have cut out the image, use a sharp craft knife to cut away the edges (fig. H). This will leave just the stamped image, which will be easier to hold when you're stamping.

7 Apply ink to the stamp and press it on a scrap piece of paper. This will allow you to see any areas that may need a little more refining.

caring for your carved stamps

When you're finished with your stamping project, your stamps will of course be covered with ink or paint. The easiest way to clean them is to gently but firmly pat your stamp with a slightly damp cloth, paper towel, or baby wipe. Avoid rubbing or scrubbing the carved stamp, or you might rub off edges or damage thin lines. Dry the stamp completely before putting it away for storage. Store it in a cool, dry paper or wooden box, with the carved side up.

stamp

The beauty of stamps is that you can use them with so many different types of inks and on so many different surfaces.

starting with the basics

All you really need to get started is an inkpad, a stamp, and paper.

1 Open the inkpad.

2 Turn your stamp over (with the carved rubber side down) and tap the stamp onto the inkpad. Rather than pushing your stamp deep into the inkpad to get it wet, tap the surface of the inkpad repeatedly until your stamp is sufficiently covered in ink. Make sure that each line and detail of the carved image is covered, so your image will come out clear.

3 Firmly press the inked side of the stamp straight down onto paper, making sure not to drag the stamp on the paper's surface. Remove the stamp by lifting straight off the paper. Don't be discouraged if your first stamped images come out smudged or uneven. Learning how to evenly apply the ink and control the stamp takes practice.

embossing

Heat embossing is a technique used to create a raised image on a piece of paper. You can use any stamp when you emboss, but you'll need to use ink that dries slowly, so you have time to add embossing powder and heat. Embossing ink, pigment ink, and VersaMark inkpads are all great choices; dye ink will dry too fast. When choosing your ink, keep in mind that the final embossed image will match the color of the embossing powder—not the ink—unless you use clear embossing powder. The last item you'll need is a heat gun.

1 Ink the stamp with your embossing or pigment ink of choice, and apply the stamp to the paper.

2 Generously sprinkle embossing powder over the stamped image, and then pour the excess powder back into the container.

3 Sweep your heat gun back and forth about 6 inches (15.2 cm) above the paper until the image starts to melt, looks shiny, and has raised edges. Take care to avoid burning your fingers on the paper.

mounting stamps

Though it's not necessary, you may choose to mount your stamps when you're finished carving them. It can be especially useful if your finished stamp is thin or flimsy, making it hard to handle. If you do feel your stamps would benefit from mounting, a simple piece of chipboard or a thin piece of wood adhered with double-sided tape or craft glue will be sufficient.

stamping tip

As you experiment with basic inking and stamping, notice that the first time you press the stamp on paper produces a very different color and effect than the second and third time you press that stamp on the paper without re-inking it. With each imprint, the color gets lighter and less opaque. Learning which imprint produces which effect allows you to have a wider range of colors to work with, from the boldest version of a color to the lightest version.

looks good on paper

When it comes to choosing stamping paper, you really can't go wrong. From scrap pieces of paper to lined notebook paper to fancy decorative paper, it's just a matter of discovering your preference.

- Many of the projects in this book will direct you to stamp on a basic blank panel card. These can be purchased at craft stores, often with coordinating envelopes.

- To make your own cards, cut a standard letter-size piece of cardstock in half. Fold each cut piece in half to make two cards that measure 4¼ x 5½ inches (10.8 x 14 cm). You can then buy standard announcement or invitation (A-2) envelopes to go with your cards.

- You can also make your own postcards by cutting standards sizes out of cardstock, usually 4 x 6 inches (10.2 x 15.2 cm) or 5 x 7 inches (12.7 x 17.8 cm). Note that unusual or square sizes will likely need extra postage, so check with your local post office if you're going to be making and mailing a lot of cards.

stamping with acrylic paint

Acrylic paint offers a vibrant, textured effect on your stamped artwork. Some artists prefer to pour the paint onto a paint palette or other flat surface before dipping the stamp into the paint. Depending on the thickness and consistency of the paint, it can be hard to ensure that the stamp is covered evenly, and this method can be quite messy. A cleaner, more precise method is to use a foam brush to coat the stamp with paint before stamping the artwork surface. Acrylic paint dries quickly, so keep that in mind whichever way you decide to adhere the paint to the stamp.

stamping on fabric

Stamps can add a touch of fun or elegance to a tote bag or T-shirt, but it's important to know the best materials and techniques to use. If your stamp has fine lines or small details, a fabric-friendly inkpad will be your best bet. Simpler or larger stamps will do well with liquid ink

stamping in layers

Some of the project images are stamped in layers, requiring several stamps to create one final image. For example, a set of stamps may include a tree trunk stamp, a branches stamp, and leaf stamps; in order to make the final tree image, you use all stamps in conjunction with each other. Pay particular attention to the colors you choose and take your time lining up the images to create the final dynamic image you are looking for.

To design your own carved stamp set, draw the complete image once, and transfer portions of it to different pieces of rubber for carving. This approach allows you to add depth and color to a single image.

With this two-layer stamp, the decoration on the mug can easily be changed.

or paint. Tightly woven fabrics will yield the best result. To prep your fabric, pre-wash and iron it so you have a clean, flat surface area to work with. Here are some pointers:

1 First, select fabric-friendly ink or paint by checking the label to see if stamping on fabric is recommended.

2 Apply ink and then stamp on the fabric just like you would on paper. Let the image dry completely before heat setting, which must be done to make it permanent.

3 To heat set the image, place a piece of parchment paper or a press cloth on top of the stamped image, and press an iron directly on top of the image for about two minutes. For best results, iron both sides of the fabric.

4 Wait at least a week before washing the fabric.

stamping on untraditional surfaces

Plastic, ceramic, or any number of other surfaces can be the target of your next stamping project. For the most part, solvent-based inks such as StazOn will work on non-porous surfaces.

Occasionally, a surface is too slick for ink to adhere, in which case you have some options. You could prep the surface by painting or collaging a few papers on it so the ink has something to stick to, or carefully stamp using ink, and then spray a clear sealer such as Krylon over your image to make it permanent.

Another material you'll occasionally see used in the projects is washi tape, which feels similar to masking tape, but with a twist—it's pretty! Washi tape can be found in a rainbow of colors and patterns to match any palette or style. You can use it for its functionality—to adhere one item to another—or you can use it purely for its aesthetic. If the surface of the tape has texture to it, you can stamp on it with permanent results; if the surface is smooth and glossy, you can try stamping it, but you may need to use a clear sealer. Washi tape can be found in any craft store, at www.Etsy.com, or even in many big box retail stores.

stamping with found objects

Even though rubber stamps are the most traditional method of stamping an image, many other objects can be used as stamps. As long as it can be inked or painted, then pressed onto a surface, it's a stamp! Stamping with found objects can produce unique images. It's an easy and earth-friendly way to reuse objects that might otherwise get thrown away.

All of the following items can be used as stamps:

- Bubble wrap: Use one bubble as a circle stamp, or use multiple bubbles for a fun background.
- Recycled cans, lids and bottle caps: They come in all sizes, and make perfect polka dots.
- Leaves or flowers: Preserve nature by stamping with it.
- Old sponges: The natural holes are sure to make for a cool background.
- Old kitchen utensils: Broken forks, potato mashers, and spatulas could all be used as stamps.

Everyday items like corrugated cardboard, paper towel tubes, flowers, leaves, and bubble wrap can be used for stamping.

handmade gift bags

Dress up even the simplest gift in one of these pretty little bags. Make several ahead of time, and you'll be ready for those occasions that call for thoughtfulness and a bit of TLC. Fill the bags with treats, tea bags, or bath soaps—whatever the recipient will love.

designer: **riyo kihara**

what you'll need

- Basic Stamping Kit, page 7
- Banner, bows, and geometric shapes templates, page 130
- Kraft paper sheets, each 12½ x 8½ inches (31.8 x 21.6 cm)
- Pigment-based inkpads in assorted colors
- Washi tape in assorted colors and patterns
- Decorative-edge scissors

instructions

make the stamps

1 Use a pencil to trace the outermost edge of the banner template onto a piece of translucent paper. For this stamp, which will print the background color, ignore the outlines of the banner.

2 Position the paper on the rubber block with the traced design facing the rubber. Rub the back side of the paper with the pencil so that the entire traced design is thoroughly transferred onto the rubber.

3 Remove the paper and carve the design.

4 Trace the banner again but this time trace the outline, which will be stamped in a darker color. Carve away the interior spaces, leaving only the outline.

5 In the same way, trace and carve the bow stamps and whatever geometric shapes you like. The primary example shown uses the bow and the circle.

stamp it

1 Use two different colors to stamp the 2-part banner at the bottom center front of the kraft paper, approximately 1½ inches (3.8 cm) from the bottom edge. Stamp the inner solid portion of the banner first, then line up the banner outline and stamp in another color (fig. A). Don't worry if the alignment isn't perfect; this will only give the stamping character.

2 Using the bows stamp and red ink, make multiple horizontal rows across the entire length of the paper, leaving room in between the rows for the next stamp.

3 Using the circles stamp with yellow ink, make multiple horizontal rows between the stamped bows. Let the ink dry completely.

4 Fold the short sides of the kraft paper toward each other so that one overlaps the other side by about ½ inch (1.3 cm). This overlapped section will be either the center back or the center front of the gift bag, depending on your preference. Tape the overlapping edge with washi tape (fig. B).

5 To make a simple flat gift bag, fold all layers along the bottom edge to one side by ½ inch (1.3 cm) and seal the fold with washi tape. Or, for a square bottom gift bag, do the following:
- Fold all layers along the bottom edge to one side by 1 inch (2.5 cm) to make a crease. Release the folds and open them up, folding the two bottom corners to form two small triangles, as shown, and pressing the folded section flat (fig. D).
- Fold the top and bottom edges of the flaps toward the center and secure in place with washi tape (figs. E & F).

6 Place your gift or message inside the bag. Trim the top edge with decorative-edged scissors (fig. C), fold it over to one side, and secure the top edge with a piece of washi tape.

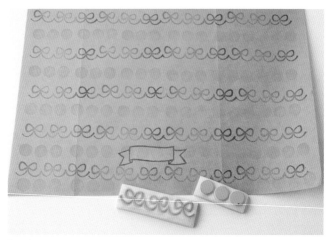

fig. A

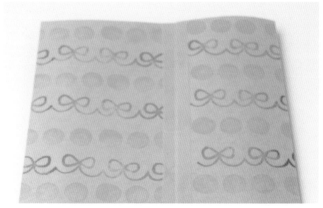

fig. B

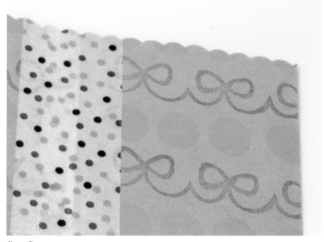

fig. C

fig. D

fig. E

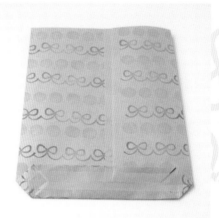

fig. F

flower pompom mobile

Stamping 14 sheets of tissue paper to make one pompom takes a bit of time, but the multi-dot stamp speeds things up, and the beautiful results are worth it!

designer: **riyo kihara**

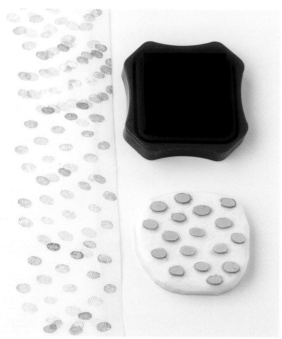

fig. A

what you'll need

- Basic Stamping Kit, page 7
- Dots template, page 131
- Dye-based inkpads in red, blue, and green
- 14 sheets of tissue paper for each pompom, each 7½ x 9 inches (19 x 23 cm)
- Baker's twine, 36 inches (91.5 cm), cut into three pieces

instructions
make the stamps

1 Use a pencil to trace the dots template onto a piece of translucent paper.

2 Position the paper on the rubber block with the traced design facing the rubber. Rub the back side of the paper with the pencil so that the entire traced design is thoroughly transferred onto the rubber.

3 Remove the paper and carve the design.

stamp it

1 Stamp the dot motif in red along both long sides (9 inches; 23 cm) of each piece of tissue paper (fig. A).

2 Stack the tissue paper, with the stamped sides facing up.

3 Fold one short edge of the stacked tissue by approximately 1 inch (2.5 cm). Fold again in the opposite direction. Keep folding back and forth until the entire stack is folded like a fan (fig. B).

4 Tie the center of the folded tissue paper with baker's twine (fig. C). Tie a loop at the opposite end of the baker's twine.

5 Cut both ends of the folded tissue to create a curved scallop shape. Carefully separate the folded tissue on both sides of the twine to allow the pompom to open up up and blossom (fig. D).

6 Repeat all steps with blue ink and green ink to make three pompoms.

7 Use the loops to attach pompoms to a hook or nail, or hang them off tree branches for festive outdoor decorations.

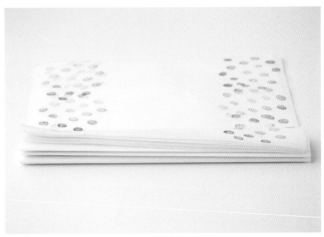

fig. B

fig. C

fig. D

geometric fabric tape

With just a bit of cotton ribbon and double-sided tape, you can make super fun fabric tape.
Cut and use the stamped tape to seal envelopes, decorate packages, or embellish journals.

designer: **riyo kihara**

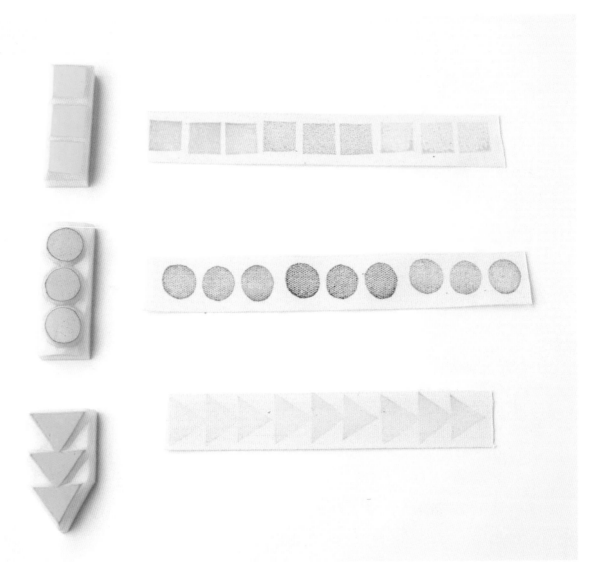

what you'll need

- Basic Stamping Kit, page 7
- Geometric templates, page 130
- Pigment-based inkpads in assorted colors
- 1 yard of cream-colored cotton ribbon, ¾ inch (2 cm) wide, cut into smaller segments
- Small towel
- Iron
- Double-sided strong-hold tape, ½ inch (1.3 cm) wide

instructions
make the stamps

1 Use a pencil to trace one of the templates onto a piece of translucent paper.

2 Position the paper on the rubber block with the traced design facing the rubber. Rub the back side of the paper with the pencil so that the entire traced design is thoroughly transferred onto the rubber.

3 Remove the paper and carve the design.

4 Repeat with the remaining templates.

stamp it

1 Stamp a geometric motif onto one of the cut segments of the ribbon, using three different inkpad colors.

2 Place a small towel on top of the stamped ribbon and press the ribbon with an iron on the highest heat setting. This will heat set the ink to ensure permanence (fig. A).

3 Remove backing from one side of the double-sided tape and adhere the tape to the back of the stamped ribbon (fig. B).

4 Trim excess ribbon or tape along the sides (fig. C).

fig. A

tips

- Vary the motifs and colors by making some strips with just one motif and one ink color, and other strips with assorted motifs and assorted ink colors.

- This method also works on silk ribbons and linen ribbons, with a slightly different look compared to the cotton ribbon.

- If you are using darker colored ribbons, use white or other light-colored inkpads.

- To make paper tape instead of ribbon, simply cut strips of kraft paper or any other paper and use the same process.

fig. B

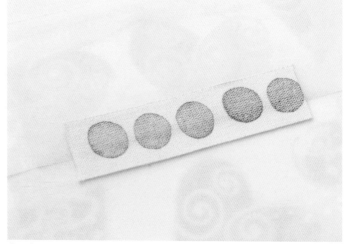

fig. C

paper snow globe

Create a small magical winter universe with this project—
where trees are laced with glitter, and snow is made of paper.

designer: **riyo kihara**

what you'll need

- Basic Stamping Kit, page 7
- Trees templates, page 131
- Mason jar, 16-ounce or larger
- Black spray paint
- Pigment-based inkpads in two shades of green
- White cardstock
- Bamboo skewers
- Origami paper in assorted colors
- Small piece of foam or hard sponge
- Multipurpose glue
- Spray adhesive
- Extra-fine glitter
- Hole punch
- Plain copy paper, 2 sheets

instructions
make the stamps

1 Use a pencil to trace one of the tree templates (or draw your own tree shape) onto a piece of translucent paper.

2 Position the paper on the rubber block with the traced design facing the rubber. Rub the back side of the paper with the pencil so that the entire traced design is thoroughly transferred onto the rubber.

3 Remove the paper and carve the design.

4 Repeat with the second tree template.

stamp it

1 Spray paint the exterior of the Mason jar's lid with black spray paint. Set aside and let dry.

2 Stamp the large and small tree multiple times with a green inkpad onto white cardstock.

3 Depending on how many final trees you decide to place in your snow globe, trim enough bamboo skewers into different lengths, anywhere between 3 to 5 inches (7.6 to 12.7 cm).

4 Glue one of the trimmed bamboo skewers to the backside of each stamped image. At the same time, glue a piece of origami paper to the back side of the stamped image so that the skewer is sandwiched in between the paper layers. Let dry.

5 Trim both layers of paper around each stamped image without being perfectly precise (fig. A). (Be sure to leave some white space around each stamped image.)

6 Cut the small piece of foam to fit on the inner ring of the Mason jar lid. This allows enough room around the foam for later screwing the jar into the lid so that it fits into the inner section of the Mason jar lid.

7 Push each skewered piece with the stamped image into the foam. Add a dot of glue where the skewer meets the foam, to ensure proper adhesion. Let dry.

8 Lightly spray a mist of spray adhesive to the standing trees. Sprinkle extra-fine glitter onto the trees.

9 Glue the entire foam piece to the inner portion of the lid. Let dry (fig. B).

10 Make a handful of confetti with plain white copy paper and a hole punch. Pour the confetti into the Mason jar.

11 Carefully insert the lid with the stamped elements into the jar and twist it closed. Turn the Mason jar upside-down and watch it snow.

fig. A

fig. B

cupcake toppers

What better way to say "thank you" than with cupcakes, personalized with cute little stamped toppers. Change the sentiment and they work equally as well for a birthday or bridal/baby shower.

designer: **riyo kihara**

what you'll need

- Basic Stamping Kit, page 7
- Foliage (2), heart, and merci templates, page 131
- Lid or other round object with a diameter approximately 2¾ inches (7 cm)
- White cardstock
- Origami paper in assorted colors and designs
- Pigment-based inkpads in brown, blue, and black
- Black fine-point marker
- Toothpicks
- Tape
- Glue
- 2 pieces of black string, each 5 inches (12.7 cm) long
- Cupcakes

instructions
make the stamps

1 Use a pencil to trace one of the templates onto a piece of translucent paper.

2 Position the paper on the rubber block with the traced design facing the rubber. Rub the back side of the paper with the pencil so that the entire traced design is thoroughly transferred onto the rubber.

3 Remove the paper and carve the design.

4 Repeat with the remaining templates.

stamp it

1 Use a lid or other round template to trace two circles onto white cardstock. Also trace two circles onto origami paper. Cut out the circles.

2 For the "merci" cupcake topper, do the following on one of the white circles:

- Using brown ink, press the single foliage stamp three times along the perimeter of the circle.
- Using black ink, stamp "merci" in the center of the circle.
- Use a black fine-point marker to add small dashes along the edge of the circle.
- Rub the edge of the circle with a blue inkpad to "frame" the work.

3 For the second cupcake topper, do the following on the remaining white circle:

- Using blue ink, press the double-foliage stamp multiple times.
- Using brown ink, stamp the heart image three times.
- Use a black fine-point marker to add small dashes and dots to outline the hearts and foliage.
- Rub the edge of the circle with a brown inkpad to "frame" the work.

4 Tape the ends of toothpicks to the backs of the stamped circles. Cover the taped ends by gluing the cut-out origami circles to the backs (fig. A).

5 Tie small lengths of black string to the toothpicks, right beneath the circles.

6 Poke the cupcake toppers into frosted cupcakes.

fig. A

choo choo train place mat

For the train lover in your life, make this fun placemat that will withstand the rigors of serious playing and serious snacking.

designer: **riyo kihara**

what you'll need

- Basic Stamping Kit, page 7
- Trains (3), tracks (2), and bush templates, page 131
- Kraft paper, approximately 16 x 12 inches (40.6 x 30.5 cm)
- Clear vinyl, approximately 16 x 12 inches (40.6 x 30.5 cm)
- Pigment-based inkpads in brown, black, and assorted greens
- Fabric placemat, approximately 19½ x 14½ inches (49.5 x 36.8 cm)
- Spray adhesive
- Sewing machine and sewing thread

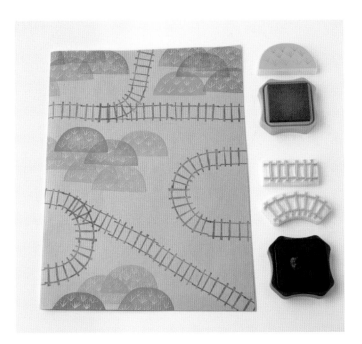

instructions
make the stamps

1 Use a pencil to trace one of the templates onto a piece of translucent paper.

2 Position the paper on the rubber block with the traced design facing the rubber. Rub the back side of the paper with the pencil so that the entire traced design is thoroughly transferred onto the rubber.

3 Remove the paper and carve the design.

4 Repeat with the remaining templates.

stamp it

1 Stamp tracks in brown ink onto kraft paper, combining curved and straight track however you like.

2 Stamp bushes in assorted shades of green ink, allowing the stamped bushes to overlap one another.

3 Use a black inkpad to stamp the three-part train set over the stamped tracks.

4 Apply spray adhesive to the back side of the stamped paper, center it, and place it onto the placemat. Place the vinyl on top of the paper.

5 Sew through all the layers of the placemat, paper, and vinyl with a sewing machine using a straight stitch close to the edges of the paper and vinyl.

geeked-out pencil pouch

Whether you sew your own pouch or buy one already made, it's easy to turn a plain fabric pouch into an uber-hip pencil pouch.

designer: **memi the rainbow**

about the pouch

Check your local craft store to find a cotton or canvas pouch. Pouches differ in style; some are zippered, some have drawstrings, some are completely blank, and some have pre-screened prints. Select the type you like and stamp according to its shape and style. Or if you have basic sewing skills, sew up your own custom pouch! The zippered pouch shown here measures 7½ x 3 inches (19 x 7.6 cm).

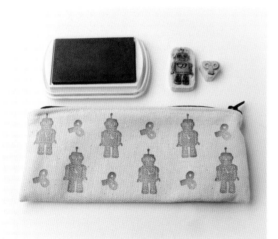

what you'll need

- Basic Stamping Kit, page 7
- Robot and crank templates, page 132
- Blank canvas pouch
- Green inkpad for fabric
- Small towel
- Iron

instructions
make the stamps

1 Use a pencil to trace the robot template onto a piece of translucent paper.

2 Position the paper on the rubber block with the traced design facing the rubber. Rub the back side of the paper with the pencil so that the entire traced design is thoroughly transferred onto the rubber.

3 Remove the paper and carve the design.

4 Repeat with the other design.

stamp it

1 Use green ink to stamp the robot multiple times onto the pouch. Allow room between the robots for the second image to be stamped.

2 Use green ink to stamp the crank multiple times between the stamped robot images.

3 Place a small towel or press cloth on top of the stamped pouch and press with an iron on the highest setting. This will heat-set the ink to ensure permanence.

4 Repeat steps 1 through 3 for the reverse side of the pouch.

tip

Rather than stamping everything in one shade of green, try a completely different color palette to jazz things up! For example, stamp the robot in blue and the crank in red.

macaroons on doilies

Hardly anyone will be able to resist these tiny and colorful treats ... especially when presented on these pretty stamped doilies.

designer: **memi the rainbow**

what you'll need

- Basic Stamping Kit, page 7
- Macaroon (2) and text templates, page 132
- Six 4-inch doilies
- Dye-based inkpads in two shades of pink and two shades of orange
- Mini macaroons

instructions
make the stamps

1 Use a pencil to trace one of the templates onto a piece of translucent paper.

2 Position the paper on the rubber block with the traced design facing the rubber. Rub the back side of the paper with the pencil so that the entire traced design is thoroughly transferred onto the rubber.

3 Remove the paper and carve the design.

4 Repeat with the other designs.

stamp it

1 Use dark pink ink to stamp the macaroon outline in the center of a doily.

2 Use light pink to carefully stamp the inner macaroon, aligning it with the stamped outline.

3 Use dark pink to stamp the text above the stamped macaroon.

4 Repeat steps 1 through 3 with two shades of orange inkpads.

5 Place mini macaroons onto non-stamped doilies. Place the stamped doilies next to the mini macaroons for a pretty presentation.

variation
Instead of doilies, substitute small brown paper bags, deli paper, or squares of parchment paper.

shrink plastic koala pendant

There's no doubt that koalas are just plain cute, and they're twice as adorable when mama and baby are shrunk down to pendant size.

designer: **memi the rainbow**

what you'll need

- Basic Stamping Kit, page 7
- Koala template, page 132
- Permanent and acid-free dye inkpad in black
- 1 sheet of transparent or white shrink plastic
- Oval scalloped craft punch, 3-inch size (7.6 cm)
- Hole punch, ⅛-inch size (3 mm)
- Paper baking sheet (parchment paper)
- Cookie sheet
- Oven
- Jump ring, 10 mm
- Needle-nose pliers
- Necklace chain

instructions
make the stamps

1 Use a pencil to trace the koala template onto a piece of translucent paper.

2 Position the paper on the rubber block with the traced design facing the rubber. Rub the back side of the paper with the pencil so that the entire design is thoroughly transferred onto the rubber.

3 Remove the paper and carve the design.

stamp it

1 Use black ink to stamp the koala image onto the shrink plastic sheet. Allow the ink to thoroughly air-dry.

2 Use a scalloped oval craft punch to punch out a frame around the stamped koala. Use the small hole punch to punch a hole at the top of the oval.

3 Set a paper baking sheet on top of a cookie sheet. Following manufacturer's instructions, set the stamped plastic oval on the baking sheet and bake in the oven. After baking is complete, allow the shrunk pendant to cool before handling.

4 Use needle-nose pliers to insert the jump ring into the punched hole, then close the ring. Attach the chain.

tips

- Carefully read the instructions on your shrink plastic box, as preparation methods and baking times differ among the various brands.

- It's important to remember that once baked, shrink plastic reduces approximately 45 percent in size.

- All plastic shapes need to be cut before going into the oven.

- Prepare several stamped and punched plastic designs that you can bake all at the same time.

cute as a covered button

You may not believe how simple it is to make your own customized covered buttons. What a great way to spice up your wardrobe!

designer: **memi the rainbow**

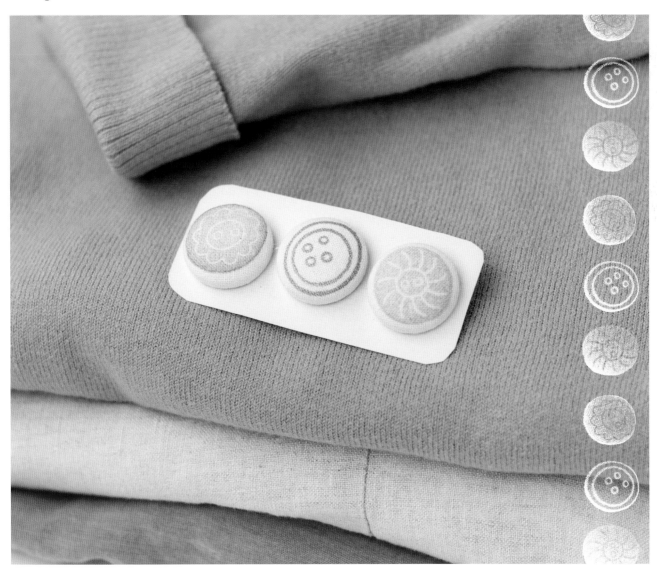

what you'll need

- Basic Stamping Kit, page 7
- Button templates, page 132
- 3 pieces of white cotton fabric scraps, cut into circles with a 2-inch (5.1 cm) diameter
- Fabric inkpads in three colors
- Small towel
- Iron
- Aluminum covered-button kit, ⅞ inch (2.2 cm) size

instructions
make the stamps

1 Use a pencil to trace a button template onto a piece of translucent paper.

2 Position the paper on the rubber block with the traced design facing the rubber. Rub the back side of the paper with the pencil so that the entire traced design is thoroughly transferred onto the rubber.

3 Remove the paper and carve the design.

4 Repeat with the other designs.

stamp it

1 Use your color of choice to stamp one of the button images in the center of one of the cut fabric circles.

2 Repeat step 1 with other colors and button images, as desired.

3 Place a small towel or press cloth on top of the stamped circles and press with an iron on the highest heat setting. This will heat-set the ink to ensure permanence.

4 Following manufacturer's instructions, sandwich the fabric pieces between the two-part aluminum buttons and snap each set together (figs. A & B).

fig. A

tips

- Make a button card by cutting cardstock into the shape of a button card, attaching covered buttons to it, and adding appropriate text.

- Liven up an old coat or sweater by replacing the buttons with stamped covered buttons.

- Add a covered button to a hat, backpack, or plain sweatshirt—any item that could use an embellishment.

fig. B

happy cutlery

Wooden cutlery not only sets a festive atmosphere, it's easy to craft with too. This project is a great way to organize and display tableware for your guests at your next picnic or outdoor party.

designer: **memi the rainbow**

what you'll need

- Basic Stamping Kit, page 7
- Face, bow, and text templates, page 132
- Wooden cutlery, for 8 to 10 place settings
- Dye-based inkpads in brown and red
- 3 Mason jars
- 3 pieces of baker's twine, 12 inches (30.5 cm) each

instructions
make the stamps

1 Use a pencil to trace the face template onto a piece of translucent paper.

2 Position the paper on the rubber block with the traced design facing the rubber. Rub the back side of the paper with the pencil

so that the entire traced design is thoroughly transferred onto the rubber.

3 Remove the paper and carve the design.

4 Repeat with the other designs.

stamp it

1 Use brown ink to stamp the face onto the upper portion of one fork, one knife, and one spoon. Note: Because the spoon has a concave shape, you will need to carefully push the face stamp firmly into the area to ensure a proper impression.

2 Use red ink to stamp the bow on the "neck" area of the fork, knife, and spoon.

3 Use brown ink to stamp the text on the handle of the fork, knife, and spoon.

4 Attach the stamped cutlery to the outside of the three jars by tying baker's twine around the tops of the jars. Fill the jars with the remaining non-stamped cutlery.

tip
To really set the mood for your party or picnic, attach a stamped knife to the invitations that you send out.

letters for lovers

Before giving your next letter or card to your beloved, adorn the envelope with a pretty little faux heart stamp. If you plan to mail your correspondence, adhere your stamp on the envelope flap and seal with a kiss.

designer: **memi the rainbow**

what you'll need

- Basic Stamping Kit, page 7
- Heart and faces templates, page 132
- Plain white paper
- Dye-based inkpads in red and black
- Postage stamp decorative-edged scissors
- Glue stick

instructions
make the stamps

1 Use a pencil to trace the heart template onto a piece of translucent paper.

2 Position the paper on the rubber block with the traced design facing the rubber. Rub the back side of the paper with the pencil so that the entire traced design is thoroughly transferred onto the rubber.

3 Remove the paper and carve the design.

4 Repeat with the face designs.

stamp it

1 Use red ink to stamp the heart onto white paper.

2 Use black ink to stamp one of the faces over the stamped heart.

3 Repeat steps 1 and 2 with the other face stamps.

4 Trim the stamped heart faces into squares, using scissors with a postage stamp decorative edge.

5 Adhere the heart stamps to envelopes using a glue stick.

variation

I liked using a red inkpad for the heart and a black inkpad for the faces. However, you can choose different colors. Remember that for the best outcome, the ink for the heart should be a lighter color than the ink for the faces.

sweet teacups on a towel

These stamps are tiny in size but huge in cuteness. Transform an ordinary dishtowel for your own kitchen, or fold one up and tie it with a ribbon for a charming hostess gift.

designer: **josephine ho**

fig. A

what you'll need

- Basic Stamping Kit, page 7
- Six-part teacup templates, page 132
- Cotton dishtowel
- Fabric inkpads in dark brown and four assorted colors
- Spare towel
- Iron

instructions
make the stamps

1 Use a pencil to trace one of the teacup templates onto a piece of translucent paper.

2 Position the paper on the rubber block with the traced design facing the rubber. Rub the back side of the paper with the pencil so that the entire traced design is thoroughly transferred onto the rubber.

3 Remove the paper and carve the design.

4 Repeat with remaining templates.

stamp it

1 Use dark brown ink to stamp the teacup. Outline several times onto the dishtowel (fig. A).

2 Use assorted colors to stamp the motifs into the teacup outlines (fig. B).

3 Place a small towel or press cloth on top of the stamped dishtowel and press with an iron on the highest heat setting. This will heat-set the ink to ensure permanence.

design tips

The dishtowel shown on page 46 came with a grid of dark blue lines. You can add grids to a plain dishtowel with embroidery stitches or fabric markers. Alternatively, stamp the teacups in a small cluster or toward the bottom edge, in a row. Feel free to make it up or branch out. You might try stamping the motifs onto cards or plain white handkerchiefs.

fig. B

lighthouse postcard

Celebrate summer with handmade nautical-themed postcards. What a great way to keep in touch with friends during vacation.

designer: **josephine ho**

what you'll need

- Basic Stamping Kit, page 7
- Three-part lighthouse, water, cloud, seagull, and nautical wheel templates, page 133
- Blank white postcards
- Dye-based inkpads in red, black, yellow, and blue

instructions
make the stamps

1 Use a pencil to trace one of the templates onto a piece of translucent paper.

2 Position the paper on the rubber block with the traced design facing the rubber. Rub the back side of the paper with the pencil so that the entire traced design is thoroughly transferred onto the rubber.

3 Remove the paper and carve the design.

4 Repeat with the remaining templates.

stamp it

1 Use black ink to stamp the lighthouse outline onto a blank white postcard.

2 Use red ink to stamp the lighthouse stripes. Align the lighthouse stripes with the stamped outline and stamp them in red.

3 Use yellow ink to stamp the light in the top of the lighthouse, then stamp the beams on both sides.

4 Stamp waves along the bottom of the postcard with blue ink.

5 Use blue ink again to stamp the nautical wheel in the upper right corner of the postcard.

6 Make additional postcards with variations by adding clouds and birds.

tip
If you want the wheel to be light in color as in the example, press the inked stamp on a scrap of paper before stamping your card.

embellished sticky notes

Ordinary sticky notes can become crafty works of art with these endearing stamps. Use the stamped notes to brighten up somebody's day.

designer: **josephine ho**

what you'll need

- Basic Stamping Kit, page 7
- Elephant, bow, boxes, rabbit, and text templates, page 133
- Sticky note pads in assorted sizes
- Dye-based inkpads in assorted colors

instructions
make the stamps

1 Use a pencil to trace the elephant template onto a piece of translucent paper.

2 Position the paper on the rubber block with the traced design facing the rubber. Rub the back side of the paper with the pencil so that the entire traced design is thoroughly transferred onto the rubber.

3 Remove the paper and carve the design.

4 Repeat with the other designs.

stamp it

1 Use an inkpad to stamp the elephant onto a sticky note. Using a different inkpad color, stamp the small bow on top of the elephant's nose.

2 Stamp the three-box stamp to create to-do check boxes.

3 Use the text stamps and the rabbit stamp in combination with the three-box stamp to make assorted designs on sticky notes.

tip

If you don't want to carve text stamps, you can buy text stamps and alphabet stamps at craft stores. Another alternative is to use a fine-point marker and letter the desired text by hand.

sticker clips

Sticker clips with small messages and shapes are just what you need to keep cards, magazines, and coupons stylishly organized.

designer: **josephine ho**

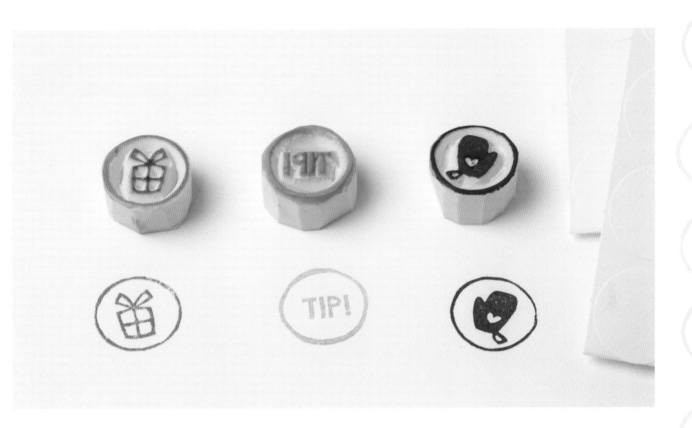

what you'll need

- Basic Stamping Kit, page 7
- Gift, mitten, spoon & fork, BUY!, TIP!, and WISH templates, page 133
- White circle label stickers, 1-inch (2.5 cm) diameter (available at office supply stores)
- Dye-based inkpads in different colors
- Paper clips in assorted colors
- Glue dots

instructions
make the stamps

1 Use a pencil to trace one of the templates onto a piece of translucent paper.

2 Position the paper on the rubber block with the traced design facing the rubber. Rub the back side of the paper with the pencil so that the entire traced design is thoroughly transferred onto the rubber.

3 Remove the paper and carve the design.

4 Repeat with the remaining designs.

stamp it

1 Using assorted colors, stamp each motif onto a pair of circle stickers.

2 Sandwich the tip of a paper clip between each pair of stamped stickers, along with a small glue dot to help adhere the stickers to the paper clip.

chameleon card

Brighten the day of someone you love with this clever card that shows how everyone is unique.

designer: **josephine ho**

what you'll need
- Basic Stamping Kit, page 7
- Chameleon templates (2), page 133
- Blank white notecard and coordinating envelopes
- Inkpads in black and assorted pale shades
- Multicolored (rainbow) inkpad
- Text or alphabet stamps

instructions
make the stamps
1 Use a pencil to trace one of the chameleon templates onto a piece of translucent paper.

2 Position the paper on the rubber block with the traced design facing the rubber. Rub the back side of the paper with the pencil so that the entire traced design is thoroughly transferred onto the rubber.

3 Remove the paper and carve the design.

4 Repeat with the other template.

stamp it
1 Use black ink to stamp the chameleon outline six times onto a blank white card.

2 Using assorted pale colors, align and stamp the solid chameleon over the stamped outlines. For one of the chameleons, use a multi-colored inkpad.

tips
- Multi-colored (rainbow) inkpads are available at craft stores and allow you to easily achieve an image with gradated colors.
- Text stamps and alphabet stamps are also available at craft stores, but an alternative is to use a fine-point marker and letter the desired text by hand.

chevron stripe hoops

Because these stamps are made with foam tape and freehand cuts, the chevron designs are slightly wonky and delightfully imperfect. Place the stamped fabrics into various-sized wooden embroidery hoops for an easy wall hanging grouping.

designer: **kerri winterstein**

what you'll need

- Basic Stamping Kit, page 7
- Double-sided foam mounting tape, three 6-inch (15.2 cm) strips
- Cardboard, 7 x 4 inches (17.8 x 10.2 cm)
- 6-inch (15.2 cm) wooden embroidery hoop
- 4-inch (10.2 cm) wooden embroidery hoop
- Spray paint in blue-green and black
- Yellow cotton fabric, 10 inches (25.4 cm) square
- Cream muslin fabric, 6 inches (15.2 cm) square
- Black solvent-based inkpad
- Paintbrush
- Blue-green acrylic paint

instructions

make the stamps

1 Draw a zigzag pattern into the three strips of double-sided foam mounting tape, then cut out the shapes.

2 Remove the paper backing from one side of the tape strips and attach them to a piece of cardboard, aligning them to create a chevron-stripe design.

3 Remove the paper backing from the front side of the mounting tape strips. Though the front side will be tacky, it will hold ink or acrylic paint with ease.

stamp it

1 Spray paint the larger hoop with blue-green paint and the smaller hoop with black paint. Set aside both to dry completely.

2 Press the chevron stamp onto a black inkpad until the stripes are fully inked. Firmly press the stamp along one edge of the yellow square of fabric. Re-ink the stamp and press another set of stripes next to the first set, carefully aligning the chevron pattern. Set aside to dry.

3 Clean the stamp with a damp rag.

4 With a small paintbrush, apply a thin layer of blue-green acrylic paint to each stripe. Center and firmly press the stamp onto the muslin fabric square. Allow to thoroughly dry.

5 Insert the yellow stamped fabric into the large blue-green hoop. Pull the fabric so it is nicely taut. Trim excess fabric as needed.

6 Insert the white stamped muslin into the smaller painted hoop. Tighten and trim the fabric as before.

bubble wrapping paper

Gift wrap can be so expensive! Discover the delight of making your own beautiful wrapping paper with a few simple items you probably already have on hand.

designer: **kerri winterstein**

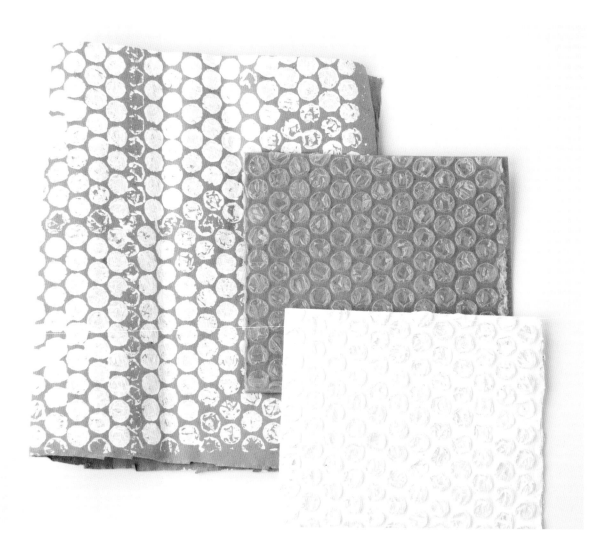

what you'll need

- Basic Stamping Kit, page 7
- Bubble wrap
- Cardboard
- Double-sided tape
- Kraft paper, large enough to wrap your gift
- Paintbrush
- White acrylic paint
- Ribbon (or stash fabric torn into strips)
- Computer-generated text on paper (optional)
- Mini wooden clothespin (optional)

instructions
make the stamps

1 Cut a square piece of bubble wrap, approximately 5 x 4½ inches (12.7 x 11.4 cm).

2 Use double-sided tape to attach the bubble wrap to a sturdy piece of cardboard that is slightly larger than the bubble wrap. When the wrap is secure, cut the cardboard down to the size of the bubble wrap.

stamp it

1 Lay out the kraft paper.

2 With a small paintbrush, apply a thin layer of white acrylic paint to the entire bubble wrap stamp. Stamp it on the kraft paper.

3 Reapply paint and repeat stamping until the entire kraft paper is covered. Allow the paper to thoroughly dry.

4 Wrap the gift with the stamped paper and tie it with ribbon. Decorate as desired, perhaps with a strip of computer-generated text attached to the ribbon with a miniature wooden clothespin.

tips

- Try using different shapes and sizes of bubble wrap to achieve different patterns.

- Experiment with a variety of paint and paper colors.

- If you don't have kraft paper, upcycle a brown grocery bag instead.

constellation and banner gift tags

Pencil stamps are easy to carve and fun to use. Make batches of these sweet tags, and keep them on hand for adorning gift boxes.

designer: **kerri winterstein**

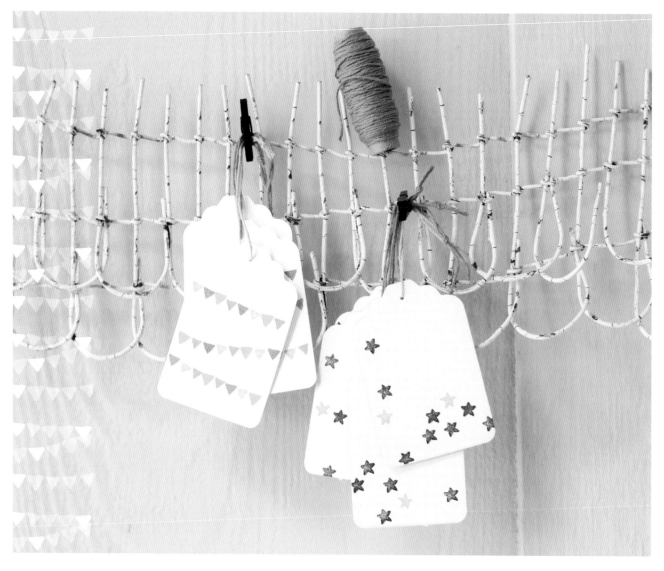

what you'll need

- Basic Stamping Kit, page 7
- 6 pencils with erasers
- Fine-point black marker
- Paper tags (available at office supply stores)
- Pigment-based inkpads in assorted colors
- 1 yard of colored string, cut into 6-inch (15.2 cm) pieces

instructions

make the stamps

1 Use a black fine-point marker to draw a star onto a pencil eraser. Draw another star on a second pencil eraser. Carve both images with a sharp craft knife.

2 Use the marker to draw a triangle onto four more pencil erasers. Carve the stamps with a sharp craft knife.

stamp it

1 Using two different ink colors, stamp a random pattern of stars onto one set of paper tags. Since you have two star stamps, use each one for a different color so you can quickly stamp the tags without cleaning the stamps between colors.

2 For the second tag design, use four different ink colors to stamp the triangles close together in horizontal rows so that they look like small banners.

3 Tie lengths of colored string to the tops of the tags.

tips

- Use these tags on your paper crafting projects, such as cards and scrapbook pages.

- Try carving other simple shapes such as hearts, stripes, and rain drops.

rings in a dish

With the right ink, you can even stamp porcelain. This simple stamped dish is just the right spot where all of your rings—both fancy and plain—can be playfully gathered together.

designer: **kerri winterstein**

what you'll need

- Basic Stamping Kit, page 7
- Ring template, page 133
- Small porcelain dish
- Black StazOn inkpad
- Matte finish spray

instructions
make the stamps

1 Use a pencil to trace the ring template onto a piece of translucent paper.

2 Position the paper on the rubber block with the traced design facing the rubber. Rub the back side of the paper with the pencil so that the entire traced design is thoroughly transferred onto the rubber.

3 Remove the paper and carve the design.

stamp it

1 Using the black StazOn inkpad, stamp the image on the inside bottom of the porcelain dish. Allow it to dry overnight.

2 Spray a thin coat of matte finish to guard against smudges and scratches. Allow to thoroughly dry.

variation
Create a thoughtful gift by carving a name or sentimental date into a stamp and printing it on a tiny dish or plate. (See page 139.)

embellished notebook

By using a very large stamp with lots of clever details, just one impression of the image is all it takes to bring this notebook to life.

designer: **ishtar olivera belart**

what you'll need
- Basic Stamping Kit, page 7
- House template, page 134
- Composition-style notebook with a recycled kraft-colored cover
- Washi tape in assorted colors and patterns
- White eyelets (2)
- Eyelet setting tools (see How to Set Eyelets, page 70)
- Dye-based inkpad in dark blue
- Stickers and cut paper shapes (clouds and raindrops shown)
- 2 pieces of baker's twine, each 12 inches (30.5 cm) long

instructions
make the stamps

1 Use a pencil to trace the house template onto a piece of translucent paper.

2 Position the paper on the rubber block with the traced design facing the rubber. Rub the back side of the paper with the pencil so that the entire traced design is thoroughly transferred onto the rubber.

3 Remove the paper and carve the design.

stamp it

1 Cover the binding of the composition book with assorted strips of washi tape. Use solid tapes and patterned tapes, including a strip of florescent pink tape.

2 Measure the right edge of the notebook to find the center. Place a dot there, approximately ½ inch (1.3 cm) from the edge. Do the same on the back edge of the notebook. Install eyelets at each marked point (see How to Set Eyelets).

3 Using dark blue ink, stamp the image to the front center bottom of the notebook.

4 Adhere stickers or fun cut-paper shapes to the top of the notebook.

5 Fold a length of baker's twine in half and knot it at one end. Thread the loose ends through the front cover eyelet and tape down the knotted end on the inside of the cover. Repeat on the other side of the notebook. Tie the ends together to secure the notebook pages.

how to set eyelets

To set an eyelet, you need the following tools, often available together in a kit in craft stores or online:

- self-healing mat
- eyelets
- hole punch to match the size of the eyelet
- hammer
- setting tool

Instructions will come with the kit, but this is the basic process:

1 Using the mat to protect the surface of your desk, lay out your tools, the eyelet, and the item to be punched.

2 Punch a hole with a hole-punching tool.

3 Insert the eyelet into the hole with the finished edge in front (fig. A).

4 Turn over the work and place the setting tool over the straight edge of the eyelet. Tap with a hammer to flatten (and thus secure) the back of the eyelet (fig. B).

fig. A

fig. B

pretty in pink postcard

One darling little rabbit image sets the stage for this simple and elegant postcard, enhanced by simple doodles and a touch of washi tape.

designer: **ishtar olivera belart**

what you'll need

- Basic Stamping Kit, page 7
- Rabbit template, page 134
- Blank postcards
- Washi tape
- Pigment-based gray inkpad
- Gel pens in orange, pink, and purple
- Glassine envelopes
- Paper confetti made from paper punches or small paper cut-outs

instructions
make the stamps

1 Use a pencil to trace the rabbit template onto a piece of translucent paper.

2 Position the paper on the rubber block with the traced design facing the rubber. Rub the back side of the paper with the pencil so that the entire traced design is thoroughly transferred onto the rubber.

3 Remove the paper and carve the design.

stamp it

1 Adhere one strip of washi tape along the bottom edge of the postcard panel. Trim any excess on the sides.

2 Using gray ink, stamp the rabbit image directly above the washi tape. Let the ink dry.

3 Add accents to the rabbit with gel pens.

4 Add doodled flowers, small dots, and a little butterfly with gel pens.

5 Place the finished postcard in a glassine envelope, and for added fun, sprinkle in some colorful paper confetti before mailing.

simply embroidered

By stamping just one fabulous rubber stamp onto a piece of fabric, you can instantly make an embroidery motif just waiting to be stitched. Accent the image with embroidery—a little or a lot—with French knot flowers and satin stitch hearts.

designer: **ishtar olivera belart**

what you'll need
- Basic Stamping Kit, page 7
- Girl template, page 134
- Piece of white fabric, 7 x 5½ inches (17.8 x 14 cm)
- Light-colored pigment-based inkpad
- Embroidery hoop
- Embroidery floss in assorted colors
- Hand embroidery needle
- Frame

instructions
make the stamps

1 Use a pencil to trace the girl template onto a piece of translucent paper.

2 Position the paper on the rubber block with the traced design facing the rubber. Rub the back side of the paper with the pencil so that the entire traced design is thoroughly transferred onto the rubber.

3 Remove the paper and carve the design.

stamp it

1 Using light-colored ink, stamp the image onto the center of the white fabric. Let the ink dry. Insert the stamped fabric into an embroidery hoop and adjust the hoop so it's taut.

2 Use assorted colors of embroidery floss and simple stitches to add embroidered decorative touches as follows:

- French knot: Eyes, nose, hair decoration, skirt pattern
- Satin stitch: Hearts

3 Cut the embroidered fabric to size to fit the frame. Remove the glass from the frame. Wrap the fabric around the glass piece and secure the back side in place with masking tape. Place the glass with the wrapped fabric back into the frame. Secure the frame's backing.

embroidery stitches
Satin Stitch

Make parallel rows of straight stitches to fill in an outline (fig. A).

French Knot

Bring the floss up through the fabric, wind it twice around the needle, hold the thread firmly, and insert the needle very close to where the floss first came up (fig. B).

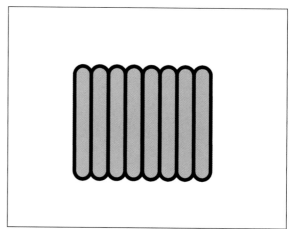

fig. A

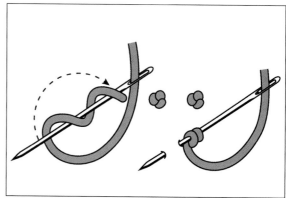

fig. B

jam jar label

Good jam deserves a great label and lets the
recipient know they're in for a real treat.

designer: **ishtar olivera belart**

what you'll need

- Basic Stamping Kit, page 7
- Label template, page 134
- Pigment-based pink inkpad
- White cardstock, 4 x 3 inches (10.2 x 7.6 cm)
- Alphabet stamps, available at craft stores and online stores in assorted sizes and fonts
- Dye-based red inkpad
- Spray adhesive
- Jar of jam
- Rubber bands
- Pink and white patterned fabric scrap, 7 inches (17.8 cm) square
- Pinking shears
- Pink baker's twine, 24 inches (61 cm)
- Washi tape in assorted colors and patterns
- Stickers or cut paper shapes
- Gluestick
- Pink paper cut into heart shapes (4)

instructions
make the stamps

1 Use a pencil to trace the tag template onto a piece of translucent paper.

2 Position the paper on the rubber block with the traced design facing the rubber. Rub the back side of the paper with the pencil so that the entire traced design is thoroughly transferred onto the rubber.

3 Remove the paper and carve the design.

stamp it

1 Use pink ink to stamp the label image onto white cardstock. Let the ink dry.

2 Use alphabet stamps and red ink to spell out the type of jam onto the cardstock. Let the ink dry.

3 Cut out the stamped label with scissors. Apply spray adhesive to the back side of the label and adhere it to the front of the jar. Burnish it well with your fingers. Place rubber bands onto the jar to ensure that the label sticks well. Set aside.

4 Lightly trace the jam jar lid in the center of the fabric scrap. Add at least 1 inch (2.5 cm) on all sides to allow for the fabric to hang over the sides of the jar. Cut the fabric into a circle with a pair of pinking shears.

5 Center the fabric on top of the lid and tie it to the jar with baker's twine.

6 Decorate the lower portion of the jam jar with strips of washi tape.

7 Remove rubber bands from the jar. Glue cut-paper shapes to the ends of the hanging baker's twine.

teapot holder

This padded holder lets you pour tea comfortably—
without burning your hand—and stylishly.

designer: **ishtar olivera belart**

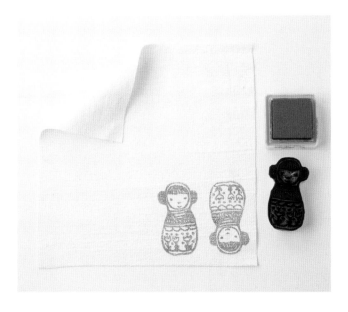

what you'll need

- Basic Stamping Kit, page 7
- Doll template, page 134
- Fabric inkpad
- White cotton fabric, 6 inches (15.2 cm) square
- Batting (or scrap flannel), 6 inches (15.2 cm) square or slightly larger
- Linen fabric for backing, 6 inches (15.2 cm) square or slightly larger
- Linen fabric for loop, 8 x 2 inches (20.3 x 5.2 cm)
- Pins
- Sewing machine and thread
- Hand-sewing needle

instructions
make the stamps

1 Use a pencil to trace the doll template onto a piece of translucent paper.

2 Position the paper on the rubber block with the traced design facing the rubber. Rub the back side of the paper with the pencil so that the entire traced design is thoroughly transferred onto the rubber.

3 Remove the paper and carve the design.

stamp it

1 Stamp the doll image in three rows onto the white cotton fabric, leaving ¼ inch (6 mm) or so on all edges for seam allowance. To fit the dolls closely together, rotate the image head-to-toe each time you stamp.

2 Place the batting square onto a work surface, followed by the linen backing fabric (right side up), followed by the stamped cotton fabric (stamped side facing down). Pin all layers along all sides (fig. A).

fig. A

fig. B

3 To make the loop, press the linen fabric strip in half lengthwise to create a center crease. Open and press both long sides toward the center crease, then refold at the center crease again. You will now have a long pressed tab that is 8 x ½ inches (20.3 x 1.3 cm). Stitch the pressed piece along the two folded edges and set aside.

4 Starting at one edge approximately 1 inch (2.5 cm) from a corner, stitch toward the corner, then around all edges with a

¼-inch (6 mm) seam allowance, stopping 2 inches (5.1 cm) from the beginning of the stitch to create an opening. Clip the corners and turn the work right side out.

5 Fold the prepared loop in half and slip it into the opening between the layers of fabric. Pin in place. Slipstitch the opening closed, making sure to work through all thicknesses, including the tab (fig. B).

thumb-stamped card

Whimsical pear-shaped abodes nestled amongst a field
of cheery fingerprint flowers set the stage for doodling
an imaginary world.

designer: **ishtar olivera belart**

what you'll need

- Basic Stamping Kit, page 7
- Pear templates, page 134
- Cardstock with white interior and blue
  exterior, cut lengthwise and folded
  into a card to measure, 4¼ x 5½ inches
  (10.8 x 14 cm)
- Matching blue envelope
- Washi tape in pink
- Pigment-based inkpads in yellow
  and pink
- Fine-point black marker
- Gel pens in pink and yellow
- Paper punches:
  - Circle, 2½ inches (6.4 cm)
  - Scallop, 3 inches (7.6 cm)
  - Cloud (optional), 1½ inches (3.8 cm)
- Translucent paper
- Glue stick

instructions
make the stamps

1 Use a pencil to trace one of the pear templates onto a piece of translucent paper.

2 Position the paper on the rubber block with the traced design facing the rubber. Rub the back side of the paper with the pencil so that the entire traced design is thoroughly transferred onto the rubber.

3 Remove the paper and carve the design.

4 Repeat with remaining pear template design.

stamp it

1 Adhere one strip of washi tape along the bottom interior edge of the card. Trim excess.

2 Punch a large circle on the lower portion of the card cover, positioning it to allow the large pear to show through the circle.

3 Cut a circle of translucent paper slightly larger than the punched circle. Center it over the punched circle and glue it in place around the outer edges.

4 Punch two scallop circles from the white/blue cardstock. Center and punch a circle from the punched scallops to create two round frames. Adhere these to the interior and exterior of the card.

5 Using yellow ink, stamp the large and small pear directly above the washi tape.

6 Use your thumbs to randomly stamp the interior of the card with yellow and pink ink. Alternate between your two thumbs and vary the angles so that the imprints have differing sizes. Let the ink dry.

7 Add doodling to the thumb stamping with a black marker and gel pens.

8 Punch a cloud shape from the white/blue cardstock or cut out a cloud shape freeform. Adhere it to the interior of the card.

9 Add thumb stamping and doodling to a corner of the envelope.

gift tag

As the old adage goes, it's the thought that counts. A thoughtfully crafted gift tag speaks volumes and can add just the right touch.

designer: **ishtar olivera belart**

what you'll need

- Basic Stamping Kit, page 7
- Flower template, page 135
- White cardstock
- Kraft-colored cardstock
- Paper punches:
  - Circle, 2½ inches (6.4 cm)
  - Scallop, 3 inches (7.6 cm)
- Purple metallic pigment-based inkpad
- Gel pen in pink
- Heart sticker
- Glue stick
- Purple eyelet
- Eyelet setting tools (see How to Make Eyelets on page 70)
- ¼-inch-wide (6 mm) ribbon, 6 inches (15.2 cm) long

instructions
make the stamps

1 Use a pencil to trace the flower template onto a piece of translucent paper.

2 Position the paper on the rubber block with the traced design facing the rubber. Rub the back side of the paper with the pencil so that the entire traced design is thoroughly transferred onto the rubber.

3 Remove the paper and carve the design.

fig. A

fig. B

stamp it

1 Punch the white cardstock with the circle paper punch. Punch the kraft-colored cardstock with the scallop paper punch.

2 Use the purple metallic ink to stamp the image onto the white circle. Let the ink dry (fig. A).

3 Add dots with a pink gel pen and attach a small heart sticker or other sticker of choice.

4 Adhere the stamped circle to the top of the scalloped circle with a glue stick.

5 Install an eyelet at the top of the tag, following the instructions on page 70 (fig. B).

6 Thread a length of pink ribbon through the eyelet and tie in place.

dressed-up envelope

The key to this project is the kraft paper envelope, which makes the stamped image and the gel pen work really pop.

designer: **ishtar olivera belart**

what you'll need

- Basic Stamping Kit, page 7
- Three Friends template, page 135
- Kraft paper envelope
- Black dye-based inkpad
- Washi tape
- Gel pens in white and blue

instructions
make the stamps

1 Use a pencil to trace the three friends template onto a piece of translucent paper.

2 Position the paper on the rubber block with the traced design facing the rubber. Rub the back side of the paper with the

pencil so that the entire traced design is thoroughly transferred onto the rubber.

3 Remove the paper and carve the design.

stamp it

1 Adhere three strips of washi tape along the bottom edge of the envelope. Trim the excess along the sides.

2 Using black ink, stamp the image directly above the top-most strip of washi tape. Let the ink dry.

3 Color in portions of the image with blue and white gel pens.

4 Add tiny random accents across the envelope with the white gel pen.

hip baby wearables

Looking for a special baby shower gift? Turn plain baby tees and snapsuits into something special, and watch the guests and mother-to-be ooh and ahh.

designer: **gertie jaquet**

what you'll need
- Basic Stamping Kit, page 7
- Birds (3), buildings (7), boats (5), and moon templates, page 135
- Black inkpad for fabric
- 2 white cotton baby wearables
- Small cotton towel
- Iron

instructions
make the stamps

1 Use a pencil to trace a bird onto a piece of translucent paper.

2 Position the paper on the rubber block with the traced design facing the rubber. Rub the back side of the paper with the pencil so that the entire traced design is thoroughly transferred onto the rubber.

3 Remove the paper and carve the design.

4 Repeat with other designs.

stamp it

1 Use black fabric ink to stamp the bird designs in a cluster onto the tee or snapsuit.

2 Place a small towel or press cloth on top of the stamped top and press with an iron on the highest heat setting. This will heat set the ink to ensure permanence.

3 Repeat steps 1 and 2 for the other baby wearables, using the buildings, boats, and moon stamps.

tip
With a stamp and fabric-friendly inkpad, you can stamp on all kinds of cotton-based wearables, including aprons, bibs, and bags.

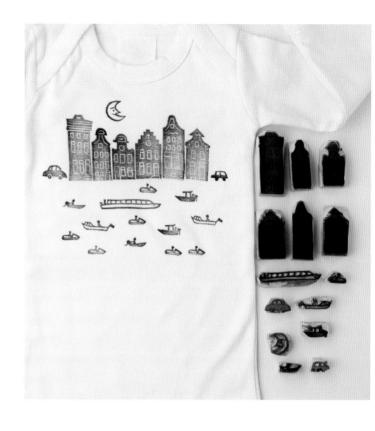

garden journal

This colorful journal is perfect for keeping notes about what you grow in your garden and how you care for your plants. Look for an existing journal with a blank cover, or make your own journal from scratch.

designer: **gertie jaquet**

make your own journal

A quick alternative to buying a journal is to make one. You'll need:

- 4 to 5 sheets of plain 8½ x 11-inch (21.6 x 27.9 cm) copy paper
- 1 sheet of cardstock, same size as the paper
- Awl
- ⅜-inch-wide (1 cm) ribbon, 1 yard (.9 m)

1 Stack the copy paper on top of the sheet of cardstock.

2 Measure 5½ inches (14 cm) across the length to find the center and fold the stack, with the cardstock on the outside for the cover.

3 Measure along the outside folded edge, 3 inches (7.6 cm) from both the top and bottom. Mark the two spots.

4 Use an awl to punch holes at both marks, through all thicknesses.

5 Thread a length of ribbon from the inside out through both holes, tie it into a bow, and trim excess.

what you'll need

- Basic Stamping Kit, page 7
- Birds (5), branches (4), wings (2), and planter templates, page 136
- Scratch paper
- Blank paper journal (or see Make Your Own Journal)
- Dye-based inkpads in black and assorted colors
- Fine-point black marker

instructions
make the stamps

1 Use a pencil to trace the planter onto a piece of translucent paper.

2 Position the paper on the rubber block with the traced design facing the rubber. Rub the back side of the paper with the pencil so that the entire traced design is thoroughly transferred onto the rubber.

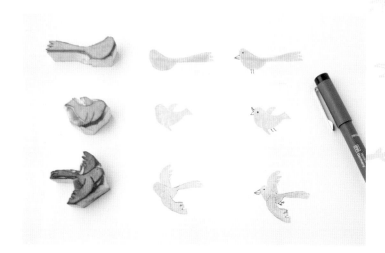

3 Remove the paper and carve the design.

4 Repeat with other designs.

stamp it

1 On scratch paper, practice stamping birds by mixing and matching the body templates and the wing templates for the birds. Decide which combinations you would like to use on the journal cover. Practice stamping the branches to make a large tree.

2 Use brown or orange ink to stamp the planter at the bottom center of the journal cover.

3 Use black ink to stamp the largest branch right above the planter image. Stamp the smaller branches to build a tree that fills up the cover.

4 Use assorted colors to stamp the various bird combinations that you practiced in step 1.

5 With a black fine-point marker, add beaks, feet, eyes, and any other details to the birds.

s'mores kit for two

Elevate your next campout (or a modern camp-in, with the aid of a microwave) by bundling up the ultimate s'mores, with this clever three-part stamped tag.

designer: **gertie jaquet**

what you'll need

- Basic Stamping Kit, page 7
- Three-part campfire templates, page 136
- Shipping tag
- Dye-based inkpads in dark blue, light blue, and yellow
- Typed or computer-generated text
- Glue stick
- S'mores supplies:
  - chocolate bar
  - graham crackers in waxed envelope
  - marshmallows in cellophane bag
- Twine, 12 inches (30.5 cm)

instructions
make the stamps

1 Use a pencil to trace one of the templates onto a piece of translucent paper.

2 Position the paper on the rubber block with the traced design facing the rubber. Rub the back side of the paper with the pencil so that the entire traced design is thoroughly transferred onto the rubber.

3 Remove the paper and carve the design.

4 Repeat with the remaining templates.

stamp it

1 Stamp the first motif (the logs and border) onto a shipping tag, using the dark blue inkpad.

2 Use the light blue inkpad to carefully stamp the second motif (the background), aligning it with the first stamped image.

3 Use the yellow inkpad to carefully stamp the third motif (the flame), aligning it with the first and second stamped images.

4 Tear or cut out the printed text and adhere it to the tag with a glue stick or simply write on the tag.

5 Gather s'mores supplies and tie them together with twine. Attach the stamped tag to the twine.

floral seed packet

Want a unique party idea? Invite the green thumbs in your life to an outdoor brunch and ask everyone to bring and exchange their bounty of seeds with one another. For the seeds you share, make these sensational seed packets for an unforgettable presentation.

designer: **gertie jaquet**

what you'll need
- Basic Stamping Kit, page 7
- Three-part flower pot templates (pot, foliage, leaves), page 136
- Letter-sized sheet of translucent paper
- Washi tape
- Dye-based inkpads in red-orange, green, and blue
- Flower seeds

instructions
make the stamps

1 Use a pencil to trace the flower pot onto a piece of translucent paper.

2 Position the paper on the rubber block with the traced design facing the rubber. Rub the back side of the paper with the pencil so that the entire traced design is thoroughly transferred onto the rubber.

3 Remove the paper and carve the design.

4 Repeat with remaining two designs.

stamp it

1 To make the seed packet:

- Cut a sheet of translucent paper in half to make two pieces that measure 5½ x 8½ inches (14 x 21.6 cm).
- Fold one of the short sides toward the middle by 3 inches (7.6 cm).
- Fold the opposite short side toward the middle by 2½ inches (6.4 cm), overlapping the first side. Adhere the edge with a piece of washi tape.
- Choose one unfolded edge as the bottom and fold it toward the folded side of the packet. Adhere the edge with a piece of washi tape.

2 Turn the packet over and stamp the motif:

- Use red-orange ink to stamp the flower pot.
- Use green ink to stamp the foliage three times, overlapping the stamped images at different angles and heights.
- Stamp the small flowers in blue ink. Allow the ink to dry completely.

3 Insert flower seeds into the envelope and fold the top side ½ inch (1.3 cm) toward the back of the packet. Adhere the edge with washi tape.

the four seasons

This art print is an elegant piece with subtle shadows created by the mounted layers. Frame and display it on an easel or hang it up to celebrate the changing seasons throughout the year.

designer: **gertie jaquet**

what you'll need

- Basic Stamping Kit, page 7
- Tree, leaf (4), and snowflake templates, page 137
- 3 pieces of watercolor paper, 4 x 6 inches (10.2 x 15.2 cm)
- 1 piece of kraft chipboard, 5 x 7 inches (12.7 x 17.8 cm)
- Dye-based inkpads in black, yellow-green, green, rust, and yellow
- Pigment-based inkpad in white
- Sharp craft knife
- Self-healing cutting mat
- Ruler
- Glue stick
- 4 sheets of black cardstock
- 1 sheet of 100-lb heavy-weight acid-free paper, 14 x 11 inches (35.6 x 27.9 cm)
- Double-sided foam tape

instructions
make the stamps

1 Use a pencil to trace the tree onto a piece of translucent paper.

2 Position the paper on the rubber block with the traced design facing the rubber. Rub the back side of the paper with the pencil so that the entire traced design is thoroughly transferred onto the paper.

3 Remove the paper and carve the design.

4 Repeat with other designs.

stamp it

1 Use black ink to stamp the tree in the center of the watercolor paper and the kraft chipboard.

2 For spring: Use yellow-green and yellow inks to stamp the smaller leaf shapes onto the branches.

3 For summer: Use dark green ink to stamp a large green leave along a tree branch. To get the lighter shade of green, make a second impression of the leaf without re-inking the stamp. Repeat this process—inking, then stamping twice—until the branches are filled with leaves.

4 For fall: Use rust and yellow inks to stamp the large leaf shape onto the branches. Stamp a few on the ground around the base of the tree.

5 For winter: Use white to stamp snow, some randomly falling from the sky, and more on the ground below the tree.

6 With a sharp craft knife, a self-healing mat, and ruler, trim all four stamped trees to measure 6 x 4 inches (15.2 x 10.2 cm).

7 Mount the stamped and trimmed trees onto black cardstock with a glue stick. Trim the black cardstock so that it is slightly but uniformly larger than the stamped panels.

8 Position the cardstock on the heavy-weight paper and trim to the desired size. Attach with double-sided foam tape.

coffee time

Whether it's coffee or tea—for two or just one—make your break time extra special with irresistible napkins.

designer: **gertie jaquet**

what you'll need

- Basic Stamping Kit, page 7
- Teapot, tea cup, sugar pot, and creamer templates, page 137
- Colored paper napkins
- Black and white pigment-based inkpads

tip

Design and carve a variety of food and beverage stamps. Print them on napkins and other items, such as paper cups or recipe cards.

instructions

make the stamps

1 Use a pencil to trace the teapot onto a piece of translucent paper.

2 Position the paper on the rubber block with the traced design facing the rubber. Rub the back side of the paper with the pencil so that the entire traced design is thoroughly transferred onto the rubber.

3 Remove the paper and carve the design.

4 Repeat with other designs.

stamp it

1 Use black ink to stamp the teapot onto one corner of a napkin.

2 Use white ink to stamp the teacup, sugar pot, and creamer next to the teapot.

3 Repeat steps 1 and 2 with additional napkins.

PINK
LEMONADE

HANDMADE SOAP

soap tissue and band

Small but thoughtful touches can make a guest feel truly welcome in your home—for instance, this bar of soap wrapped in tissue and a stamped band. Have one in the guest bath to welcome overnight guests.

designer: **noelle griskey**

PINK
LEMONADE

HANDMADE SOAP

what you'll need

- Basic Stamping Kit, page 7
- Lemon template, page 137
- Bar of soap
- Light pink tissue paper
- White gel pen
- White cardstock with computer-generated text
- Dye-based dark pink inkpad
- Sharp craft knife
- Self-healing cutting mat
- Ruler
- Tape or sticker

instructions
make the stamps

1 Use a pencil to trace the lemon template onto a piece of translucent paper.

2 Position the paper on the rubber block with the traced design facing the rubber. Rub the back side of the paper with the pencil so that the entire traced design is thoroughly transferred onto the rubber.

3 Remove the paper and carve the design.

stamp it

1 Wrap a bar of handmade or store-bought soap with tissue paper.

2 Make white polka dots on the tissue paper with a white gel pen.

3 Cut the cardstock with the computer-generated text into a long strip that measures 7 x 1½ inches (17.8 x 3.8 cm).

4 Use the dark pink inkpad to stamp the lemon image directly above the text. Let the ink dry completely.

5 With the strip face down, place the soap onto the band and determine where the folds will be when you wrap the strip around the bar. Lightly score the strip at these determined spots with a ruler and a sharp craft knife. This will ensure smooth and even folds.

6 Wrap the band around the soap and attach with a piece of tape or a sticker.

computer-generated text

To make computer-generated cardstock, determine the measurements for your soap band based on the size of the bar of soap that you are using. The soap shown here measures 3 x 2 x 1 inches (7.6 x 5.1 x 2.5 cm) and the band measures 7 x 1½ inches (17.8 x 3.8 cm). Determine where on the band you would like for the text to be, keeping in mind where the folds will be on the band. Type the desired text, print out, and cut. Experiment a few times with regular copy paper before you actually print the text out onto cardstock.

PINK
LEMONADE

HANDMADE SOAP

baby gift ribbon and card

No matter how special the actual gift, the mother-to-be will equally treasure this wonderful presentation with coordinating ribbon and card.

designer: **noelle griskey**

what you'll need

- Basic Stamping Kit, page 7
- Chick template, page 137
- Light-blue cotton fabric, enough to cut a strip, 40 x 2 inches (101.6 x 5.2 cm)
- Pinking or fabric shears
- Yellow inkpad for fabric
- Small towel
- Iron
- Sewing machine (optional)
- Sheet of cardstock
- Sharp craft knife
- Self-healing cutting mat
- Ruler
- Light blue paper, 6 x 1½ inches (15.2 x 3.8 cm)
- Glue stick

instructions
make the stamps

1 Use a pencil to trace the chick template onto a piece of translucent paper.

2 Position the paper on the rubber block with the traced design facing the rubber. Rub the back side of the paper with the pencil so that the entire traced design is thoroughly transferred onto the rubber.

3 Remove the paper and carve the design.

stamp it: gift ribbon

1 Cut the 40 x 2-inch (101.6 x 5.2 cm) fabric strip.

2 Using a yellow inkpad, stamp the chick onto the fabric strip in a repeating pattern from one end to the other.

3 Place a small towel on top of the stamped strip and press with an iron on the highest heat setting. Repeat until the entire strip has been pressed. This will heat set the ink to ensure permanence.

computer-generated text

To make computer-generated cardstock, determine the measurements for your gift card. The gift card shown here measures 3 inches (7.6 cm) square. Determine where on the card you would like for the text to be, keeping in mind where the fold will be on the card. Type the desired text, print out, cut and fold. Experiment a few times with regular copy paper before you actually print the text out onto cardstock.

4 Wrap the gift with newsprint paper and tie the gift with the stamped ribbon. Note: If the gift you are wrapping is larger than the ribbon is long, make additional strips of ribbon and connect two of the ends with a sewing machine to make one long strip.

stamp it: gift card

1 Type a sentiment using a computer and print it out on cardstock (see Computer-Generated Text).

2 Cut the computer-generated cardstock to measure 3 x 6 inches (7.6 x 15.2 cm), using a sharp craft knife, cutting mat, and ruler.

3 Lightly score the card in the middle using a ruler and sharp craft knife. Fold the card along the scored line for a clean edge.

4 Wrap the band of light blue paper around the upper portion of the folded card, creasing it along the card's crease. Adhere with a glue stick.

5 Use the yellow inkpad to stamp the chick image onto the blue paper band. Let the ink dry completely.

6 Add the card to the wrapped gift by tucking it beneath the stamped ribbon.

cutting edge
Use pinking shears to cut the fabric strip on all edges to prevent it from fraying. However, if you like the frayed look, use regular scissors.

tips
- Light-colored fabrics and paper in other shades like pink, green, and cream would also work well for this project.

- Stamp directly onto plain giftwrap to make quick and easy patterned wrapping paper.

office supply boxes

This stamped duo is a handsome way to corral small office supplies like paper clips and pushpins.

designer: **noelle griskey**

what you'll need

- Basic Stamping Kit, page 7
- Pushpin and paper clip templates, page 137
- White cardstock, large enough to cover the box lids
- Dye-based inkpads in primary colors
- Square papier-mâché box, 4½ inches (11.4 cm) square
- Round papier-mâché box, 4½ inches (11.4 cm) in diameter
- Glue stick or craft glue

instructions
make the stamps

1 Use a pencil to trace the pushpin template onto a piece of translucent paper.

2 Position the paper on the rubber block with the traced design facing the rubber. Rub the back side of the paper with the pencil so that the entire traced design is thoroughly transferred onto the rubber.

3 Remove the paper and carve the design.

4 Repeat with the paper clip template.

stamp it

1 Stamp the pushpin image onto a piece of white cardstock, using assorted inkpads in primary colors. Allow the repeating pattern to look random and playful. Clean the stamp before changing ink colors (see Caring for Your Carved Stamps, page 10).

2 Repeat step 1, this time stamping the paper clip image onto a separate sheet of cardstock.

3 Trim the pushpin-stamped cardstock so it is slightly smaller than the lid of the square papier-mâché box.

4 Trim the paper clip-stamped cardstock so it is slightly smaller than the lid of the round papier-mâché box.

5 Adhere each trimmed cardstock to the top of the matching lid.

about the box

Plain boxes made from papier-mâché look like they are made from smooth brown cardboard. They are inexpensive and available at craft stores, artist supply stores, and online. Each box is a "blank canvas" just waiting to be decorated.

wine furoshiki

In Asian cultures, furoshikis are traditional wrapping cloths used to elevate the presentation of all sorts of gifts. When giving a bottle of wine to a friend, transform a plain flour sack into a colorfully stamped furoshiki, and use it to wrap and present the gift.

designer: **noelle griskey**

what you'll need

- Basic Stamping Kit, page 7
- Wine bottle templates (2), page 137
- White standard cotton flour sack towel
- Fabric inkpads in brown and wine
- Small spare towel
- Iron
- White cardstock, trimmed to 3 inches (7.6 cm) square
- Hole punch
- Thin ribbon, 7 inches (17.8 cm) long
- Bottle of wine

instructions
make the stamps

1 Use a pencil to trace one of the wine bottle templates onto a piece of translucent paper.

2 Position the paper on the rubber block with the traced design facing the rubber. Rub the back side of the paper with the pencil so that the entire traced design is thoroughly transferred onto the rubber.

3 Remove the paper and carve the design.

4 Repeat with the second template.

stamp it

1 Find the center of the towel and use the brown inkpad to stamp the smaller wine bottle in the center. Be sure to stamp on a protected work surface, as the ink will seep through the flour sack towel.

2 Use the wine inkpad to stamp the larger wine bottle right next to the first stamped image.

3 Stamp a row of double wine bottles along the center, with each pair spaced approximately 2 inches (5.1 cm) apart.

fig. A

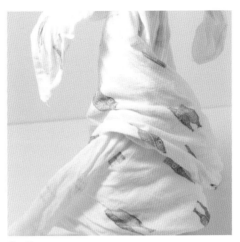

fig. B

fig. C

fig. D

4 After the first row has been stamped, turn the towel so the stamped images are upside down. Stamp another row of double wine bottles that are right-side up, staggered, and about 2 inches (5.1 cm) away from the first stamped row.

5 Continue turning and stamping the fabric, making rows until the entire towel has been stamped.

6 Place a small towel on top of the stamped flour sack and press with an iron on the highest heat setting. Repeat until the entire sack has been pressed. This will heat-set the ink to ensure permanence.

7 Wrap the bottle of wine as follows:
- Spread the towel on a flat surface with the stamped side facing down.
- Place the wine bottle standing up, right at the center of the towel.

- Pull two opposite corners together and tie very tightly at the top of the bottle (fig. A).
- Take the two remaining (untied) corners and wrap them around the body of the wine bottle so that it looks like the corners are hugging the bottle. Tie these ends together twice (figs B & C).
- Tie the very tips of the first two corners twice very tightly, to create a carrying handle (fig. D).

8 Following the same motif, stamp the two wine bottle images in brown and wine color onto the trimmed cardstock.

9 Punch a hole at the corner of the cardstock and thread the length of thin ribbon through the hole. Tie the ribbon to the front knot of the furoshiki.

simply impressive gift wrap

A simple, elegant floral stamp can do wonders for a bit of kraft paper. The presentation of a gift can be as important as the gift itself, and this project has you covered.

about the contributors

Gertie Jaquet is a children's book illustrator living in the Netherlands who loves to make stamps, take photos, and travel. She often organizes stamp-carving workshops to share her love of stamp making. To learn more about her, visit *www.astampaday.blogspot.com*.

Cynthia Shaffer is a mixed-media artist, quilter, and creative sewer. She is the author of Stash Happy Patchwork (Lark, 2011) and Stash Happy Appliqué (Lark, 2012). Cynthia lives in Orange, California, with her husband, Scott; her sons, Corry and Cameron; and their beloved Boston Terriers. To learn more about her, visit *www.cynthiashaffer.com*.

Josephine Ho hails from Singapore, where she picked up rubber stamping in 2006 and hasn't stopped since. Stamping at night once her kids have gone to sleep, she is particularly inspired by the simplicity and zen-like quality of Japanese designs. To learn more about her, visit *www.lovesprouts.blogspot.com*.

Kerri Winterstein is a twenty-something wife, mama, and creative soul. She currently divides her time between dreaming up new products for her Etsy shop, living the adventures of mommyhood, and striving for simplicity. To learn more about Kerri, visit *www.yourwishcake.com*.

Patricia, also known as **Memi the Rainbow**, is an Italian girl living in Paris, where she is attending art school. The city of Paris is her main source of inspiration, and since she's moved there, she's discovered that she's a compulsive crafter with an obsession for rubber stamps. To learn more about her, visit *www.memitherainbow.blogspot.com*.

Noelle Griskey is originally from Los Angeles, but now resides in Pittsburgh, PA, by way of Portland, OR, and Washington, DC. Working from her home studio, she creates a line of hand-printed paper goods. When she's not creating, she loves gardening, cooking, photography, and travel. To learn more about Noelle, visit *www.pinkbathtub.com*.

Riyo Kihara is a full-time rubber stamper living in Yamaguchi, Japan. She also enjoys making jewelry and felting. Always eager to learn a new skill, she recently began teaching herself to sew. To learn more about Riyo, visit *www.talktothesunhandmade.blogspot.com*.

Sarah K. Patro is a South Jersey native living in Scottsdale, AZ, with her husband and golden retriever, Ollie. She has been creating stamps through her shop, Creatiate, since December 2010, and she has recently opened up a second shop, impression ONE, which focuses on hand-carved linocut art prints. To learn more about her, visit *www.creatiate.etsy.com*.

ishtar olivera belart is an illustrator from Spain, whose love for art began at an early age. She has illustrated children's books and designed rubber stamps for Penny Black, and she also teaches craft workshops. She is currently living in England, where she enjoys taking walks through the forest with her two sons, Tuti and Keni. To learn more, visit *www.ishtarolivera.com*.

editor: **jenny doh**
writer: **amanda crabtree weston**
copyeditor: **nancy d. wood**
assistant editors:
  kerri winterstein, jennifer taylor, monica mouet
art director: **kristi pfeffer**
graphic designer: **raquel joya**
photographer: **cynthia shaffer**
cover designer: **kristi pfeffer**

about the author

Jenny Doh is the head of *www.crescendoh.com* and a lover of art. She has authored and packaged numerous books including *Creative Lettering*, *Journal It!*, *We Make Dolls*, *Hand in Hand*, and *Signature Styles*. She lives in Santa Ana, California and loves to create, stay fit, and play music.

index